W9-BBX-753

Smokejumpers

Battling the Forest Flames

by Diana Briscoe

Reading Consultant:
Timothy Rasinski, Ph.D.
Professor of Reading Education
Kent State University

Content Consultant:
Mike McMillan
Smokejumper
spotfireimages.com

Capstone Curriculum Publishing

Capstone Curriculum Publishing materials are published by Capstone Press, P.O. Box 669, 151 Good Counsel Drive, Mankato, Minnesota, 56002
http://www.capstone-curriculum.com
http://www.capstone-press.com

Library of Congress Cataloging-in-Publication Data
Briscoe, Diana, 1949–
    Smokejumpers: battling the forest flames/by Diana Briscoe.
        p. cm.—(High five reading)
    Includes bibliographical references (p. 46) and index.
    Summary: Looks at the history, equipment, training, and work of fire fighters who parachute into wildfires burning in areas that are otherwise hard to reach.
        ISBN 0-7368-9526-4 (pbk.)—ISBN 0-7368-9548-5 (hardcover)
        1. Smokejumpers—Juvenile literature. 2. Wildfire fighters—Juvenile literature. [1. Smokejumpers. 2. Wildfire fighters. 3. Fire fighters.]
I. Title. II. Series.
SD421.23 .B75 2002
634.9'618—dc21

                                2002000187

Created by Kent Publishing Services, Inc.
Executive Editor: Robbie Butler
Designed by Signature Design Group, Inc.

Photo Credits:
Cover, pages 7, 8, 10, 12, 14–15, 19, 23, 25, 26, Mike McMillan/Spotfire Images; page 4, AFP/Corbis; page 16, Michael Pole/Corbis;
page 17, Bureau of Land Management/NIFC; page 20,
Michael S.Yamushita/Corbis; page 28, Underwood & Underwood/Corbis;
page 34, Raymond Gehman/Corbis

Printed in the United States of America.

1 2 3 4 5 6 08 07 06 05 04 03

Table of Contents

CHAPTER 1

Call to Action

Are they brave? Or are they just crazy? Each year, more than 450 men and women wait for orders to jump from planes to fight forest fires. Their daring saves our homes and forests from fires. But what type of person does this?

Smokejumpers in their jumpsuits

Waiting for the Call

At every smokejumper base, a plane sits on the runway. Gear is stacked neatly in piles around the plane. Jumpsuits hang from "speed racks" inside the base. Nearby, smokejumpers wait for the call to action.

The office phone rings. A siren sounds. Moments later, the spotter comes out. "Suit up, folks! We're heading out."

Quickly, the smokejumpers climb into their kevlar jumpsuits. The group runs to the plane. Each smokejumper puts on a helmet. Each one straps on two parachutes —a main chute and a reserve chute. The group help each other with their gear and do safety checks. From first call, the team tries to be in the air in six minutes.

The plane rumbles down the runway. Another mission has begun!

---

jumpsuit: a suit that parachute jumpers wear
spotter: the person in command of a smokejumper team
kevlar: a special fireproof material
parachute: a long piece of fabric attached to thin ropes
reserve: spare; backup
mission: a special job or task

On the Way

It is loud inside the plane. There is little talk. A smokejumper once said, "You're working up a pretty good sweat inside the jumpsuit. You're very apprehensive, very focused. . . . You think about the mission at hand, the jump."

Smokejumpers wear a shirt and heavy Nomex pants under their jumpsuit. They also wear heavy work boots. Smokejumpers supply their own boots. They must also supply one knife and a watch.

Each smokejumper carries a gear bag. This bag holds gloves, a hard hat, a water bottle, and other personal items. Each has a let-down rope in one jumpsuit pocket. If stuck in a tree, the jumper uses this rope to rappel to the ground.

---

apprehensive: highly aware
focused: thinking only about one thing
Nomex: a material that can stand heat
rappel: to use ropes to let yourself down from a high place

The Parachute

Forest Service smokejumpers always
use a round parachute and a static line.
Jumpers with the Bureau of Land
Management use the square or "ram-air"
parachute. This chute is easier to steer.

Ram-air parachutes are easier to steer.

---

static line: a rope that opens the parachute as a jumper
leaps from a plane

Smokejumpers practice their jumping skills.

Getting Ready to Jump

The plane reaches the fire. The spotter looks for an area to jump that is free of trees, brush, and rocks. He throws long streamers from the plane. As they drift, the streamers show the wind speed and direction. This helps the spotter tell which way the wind will carry the smokejumpers.

The spotter chooses a jump site. When the spotter commands, the smokejumpers begin to jump from the plane. As their parachutes open, the smokejumpers float toward the ground.

A load of smokejumpers has eight to 10 members. The plane makes as many passes as needed to give everyone time to jump safely.

---

streamer: a long piece of narrow paper that is rolled up
pass: the act of going by, beyond, over, or through

The Jump

Smokejumpers jump from either 1,500 or 3,000 feet (457 or 914 meters). This depends on the parachutes they use. Once they jump, they have only about five seconds to fix any problems. If the main chute has problems, the reserve chute will usually get them down safely. Since 1940, only four smokejumpers have died jumping.

A smokejumper trains to escape from a tree.

The Landing

Landing in a forest area is tricky. A smokejumper is trained to escape if stuck in a tree. The other jumpers will give advice from the ground. If the jumper is not in danger, the advice may not be so helpful! Sometimes there is more joking than helping.

Supplies Come Next

The plane makes a pass at about 150 to 300 feet (46 to 91 meters) to drop cargo boxes. These boxes contain tools, more water, and food. Some missions will last more than 24 hours. For these missions, the boxes also contain sleeping bags.

The drop must be exact. Strong winds can blow the boxes off target. Then the crew has to trek cross-country to find them.

---

cargo: things carried by a truck, plane, train, or ship
target: a mark to aim at
trek: to walk across difficult ground

CHAPTER 2

On the Ground

You can smell the smoke. Your eyes begin to burn. In the distance, you hear the crackle of flames. Nearby, firefighters black with smoke shout greetings. Your group is the backup team they've been waiting for.

Smokejumpers cut a fireline.

Fighting the Fire

Smokejumpers are firefighters. Their goal is to fight small fires before they become big fires. To do this, smokejumpers cut a fireline around the fire so the fire won't spread.

To cut a fireline, *sawyers* use chain saws to cut down trees and bushes. Other firefighters called *pullers* or *swampers* place the cut matter on the *green*. This is the side of the fireline where the fire is not burning. The burning side is called the *black*.

Scrapers or *diggers* then use shovels and a special tool called a *pulaski* (pul-LASS-kee). This tool has an ax blade on one side and a hoe blade on the other. Scrapers or diggers chop and scrape shrubs, grass, and roots. This removes possible fuel for the fire.

Sometimes firefighters use a "direct attack." They go really close to the fire. Then they knock down and scrape away the fuel that feeds it.

---

fireline: land specially prepared to stop a fire from spreading
fuel: something that gives heat or power by burning

Backfires Burn and Clear

Another firefighting tactic is to light a backfire. A backfire is a fire the firefighters start on purpose. It burns and clears an area between a control line and the wildfire. A control line can be a road or river. When the wildfire reaches this cleared area, it runs out of fuel. Firefighters often light backfires in places where wildfires move quickly.

---

tactic: a means to reach a goal

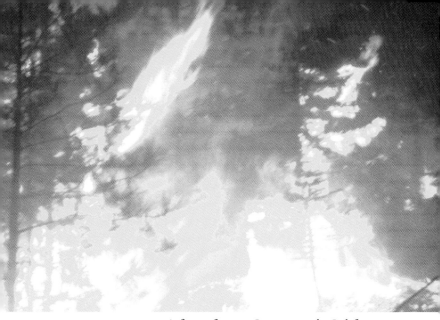

A forest fire in Cottonwood, California

Drought Means Danger

About 100,000 wildfires occur every year in the western United States and Alaska. These fires tend to be much worse in drought years.

A drought kills trees and plants. Dead trees and plants make more fuel for fires. A lack of rain also leads to lower humidity. This dries out even living trees and plants. Dry leaves and wood burn more easily.

---

drought: a severe lack of rain
humidity: the amount of water vapor in the air

Air Tankers and Helicopters

In a city, people often use water to fight fires. Smokejumpers may be able to use water if a lake or river is near the fire. Smokejumpers then can use pumps and hoses to draw water from the lake or river.

But water can be hard to find in the forest. Then firefighters may use portable tanks to hold and carry water. Helicopters and trucks haul water to fill large tanks. Then firefighters fill and carry smaller tanks on their backs to pump water on the fire.

A helicopter dumps water on a fire.

portable: able to be carried or moved easily

An air tanker dumps fire retardant.

Helicopters can also bring water directly to the fire. A chopper can carry a 100- to 3,000-gallon (379- to 11,356-liter) bucket hung from below. This bucket has a trip line. The trip line opens the bucket. Water in the bucket then pours onto the fire.

Air tankers can carry large loads of fire retardant. The retardant is dumped over an area to coat the plants and trees. This coating can stop or slow down flames.

---

trip line: a rope or cord used to open a latch on a door
fire retardant: a chemical that slows the advance of a fire

Why Do Wildfires Start?

Lightning starts most wildfires. But human carelessness, and sometimes human malice, can also start them. Too often, campers and walkers leave litter behind. A broken bottle can focus sunlight onto dry leaves or twigs. Within minutes, a fire can start. A driver may toss a cigar from a passing car. That cigar may start a fire that destroys both life and property.

The End of the Job

Some firefighters stop fighting a fire when it is almost under control. Others stay and search for hot spots underground. This may take from two days to a month or more.

Once they are done, smokejumpers have to carry out all their gear. This includes all the gear from the cargo boxes. Each smokejumper may carry a load that weighs more than 100 pounds (45 kilograms).

---

malice: a desire to hurt someone or something
focus: to aim rays of light through a lens
hot spots: areas where roots under the soil are burning

Sometimes smokejumpers get a ride out. Choppers may pick them up. Or they may ride on a fire engine. Four-wheel-drive fire engines can go far into the forest along dirt roads.

If smokejumpers must hike out, it's hard work. But many don't mind. They enjoy the beauty of the forest. They also enjoy hiking with friends who share the feeling of pride in a job well done.

Smokejumpers hike out.

Chapter 3

Training Camp

You are fit. Or so you think. You're a skilled firefighter. Or so you think. But now it's crunch time. You're trying out to become a smokejumper. Are you prepared enough to make it?

Smokejumpers in training try to get out of their parachutes in a swimming pool.

Basic Requirements

In the United States, smokejumpers must be U.S. citizens. They must be at least 18 years old. Every candidate must pass a complete medical check-up. Smokejumpers may spend 14 to 16 hours per day digging firelines. So they must be fit. Good eyesight and hearing are also required.

To qualify for smokejumper training, candidates must first work at least one season (90 days) in forestry or agriculture. They usually have at least a high school diploma. If they do not, they must first work for a full year in farming or forestry.

Lastly, candidates need at least one season of forest fire fighting. Oddly, they should not have any parachute training. True beginners won't have any bad habits!

---

citizen: a person who belongs to a named country
candidate: someone who wants to join a group
medical: anything to do with health and medicine
qualify: to reach a level that allows you to do something
forestry: working with trees, woodlands, and forests
agriculture: farming of all types

The First Week

Every winter, people apply for smokejumper rookie training. Once chosen, candidates spend four to six months getting in shape. They need to work out nearly full-time to prepare.

Rookie training starts in April, May, or June. On the first day, candidates must pass a physical test. This includes seven pull-ups, 25 push-ups, 45 sit-ups, and a run of 1.5 miles (2.4 kilometers). Rookies must complete the run in less than 11 minutes. Most pass this test easily.

During the week, rookies must do two pack-out tests. For one test, they carry 110 pounds (50 kilograms) over a flat, 3-mile (4.8-kilometer) course. They must finish the course in less than 90 minutes. In the second test, they carry 85 pounds (39 kilograms) over 2.5 miles (4 kilometers) of hilly, broken ground.

---

rookie: a person who is new to a job
physical: anything to do with the body
pack-out test: a test to carry a heavy load over a distance

That's Not All!

Rookies do calisthenics and run several times a day. This tough training makes it hard to pay attention during the classroom work they must do.

Rookies also must show they can handle maps, chain saws, water pumps, and other tools. A rookie who fails any training unit is dropped from the program.

Could you carry a heavy pack on a rugged mountain trail?

calisthenics: a type of exercise to make certain parts of the body stronger

23

The Second Week

In week two, rookies jump from a 40-foot (12-meter) shock tower to learn how to exit planes. They also practice "let-downs" from a platform. This teaches them what to do when their parachutes snag in a tree.

Rookies use a landing simulator to learn parachute landing rolls. They practice finding cargo boxes. They also learn to use spurs and a rope to climb trees.

Rookies learn aircraft safety. They must pass a test on all safety rules. Again, one failure wipes them out of the program.

Lastly, rookies must complete an obstacle course. Picture a 7-foot (2.1-meter) wall next to monkey bars. That's just part of the course. The course also has tires, ramps, and a rope. Could you handle all those?

---

snag: to catch or grab
simulator: a machine that gives you an experience that is like the real thing
spur: a spike on the heel or bottom of a boot
obstacle: something that gets in your way or prevents you from doing something

A rookie jumps from a shock tower.

Finally—Jump!

At the end of rookie training, candidates make seven parachute jumps. First, they make a jump into an open field. Then the jumps get harder. The seventh jump is into a small clearing circled by tall trees. It takes training, confidence, and skill to land on target.

A candidate makes a practice jump.

confidence: belief in your abilities

Always Busy

If accepted, the new smokejumper gets a temporary contract. This first contract is a trial. It lasts for one season, not more than 180 days. If hired for a second season, the jumper gets a longer contract.

Smokejumpers work hard. They must stay very fit. Their schedule includes a 60- to 90-minute daily workout. They also have chores at the base. They pack cargo boxes. They check and repack parachutes. They do housekeeping.

Sometimes, smokejumpers are sent to area Ranger Districts. This happens only when there are few fires to fight. At Ranger Districts, smokejumpers may clear grass and brush to reduce fuel for fires. They may also repair trails and build fences.

Smokejumpers also may be sent to other places to help fight fires. This happens in bad fire years.

---

temporary: not lasting; having an end

Chapter 4

The First Smokejumpers

In 1940, the Forest Service tested metal bombs filled with water to fight fires. They dropped these bombs from planes onto fires. The bombs didn't work. So they tried parachute jumps. That's when smokejumpers first went into action. The rest is history!

Lieutenant Nick B. Mamer

Airplanes over the Forests

In 1918, Henry A. Graves had a bright idea. The head of the U.S. Forest Service asked the Army Air Service if he could borrow some planes and pilots. He wanted to make air patrols to spot fires from the air.

The first pilot to do this was Lieutenant Nick B. Mamer. He had flown in France during World War I (1914–18). Mamer and Forest Inspector Howard R. Flint began to take aerial photos of wildfires. In 1929, they started to make cargo drops to firefighters.

In 1935, the Aerial Fire Control Experimental Project was set up. This project dropped water and chemicals onto wildfires.

---

aerial: from the air
experimental: something that has not yet been fully tested
chemical: a substance used in chemistry

Jumping to Fight Fires

In 1934, the Forest Service made some test jumps. They wanted to see if firefighters could land safely in a forest. But the Forest Service decided this was too risky. They gave up on the idea for a time.

In 1939, some professional parachute jumpers made more test jumps in Washington. Some Forest Service staff also made their first jumps. Walt Anderson, a staff member, was among them. He came up with the name *smokejumpers*.

In 1940, the Forest Service began to choose the first smokejumper candidates. There were 15 in the group. Only two candidates completed all 10 training jumps.

---

professional: someone who is paid to do a job that requires special training

First to the Attack

The first men to jump near an actual forest fire were Rufus Robinson and Earl Cooley. They made their historic jump at Marten Creek in Nez Percé Forest. The date was July 12, 1940.

Smokejumpers Francis Lufkin and Glen Smith pose for this picture in 1940.

---

historic: a past event that is seen as important

Another Way to Serve?

The United States entered World War II in 1940. Not everyone thought it was right to fight in a war, however. In fact, more than 70,000 young men refused to join the military. They were called *conscientious* (con-shee-EN-chus) *objectors* or COs. Many of these men served their country in other ways.

One CO, Phil Stanley, was working on a fire and trail crew in 1942. He heard that the smokejumper service was about to close. Nearly all the young, fit men had gone to war. That included smokejumpers. So Stanley told the Forest Service that COs could serve as smokejumpers. When the Forest Service agreed, more than 300 COs signed up.

---

conscientious objector: a person who refuses to do something because his or her beliefs forbid it

COs Made to Leave

Many of the Forest Service staff hated the idea of COs as smokejumpers. The staff was angry that COs would not join the war. One staff member, Earl Cooley, said some staff thought that "the COs should be treated like dogs . . . . At the same time, they expected them to give 100 percent effort."

When the war ended, the Forest Service did not keep any of the CO smokejumpers. Some COs had become bosses or teachers on the jumping teams. Soon war veterans would want to become smokejumpers. Some Forest Service staff thought these veterans would not like to have a CO as a boss or a teacher.

veteran: a person who served in the military

— CHAPTER 5 —

Trapped in Fire

Smokejumpers face many dangers. They come very close to fires. Yet very few jumpers have died fighting fires. Why do you think they have such a good record?

Firefighters plan an escape route from the ridge of a canyon.

Fire on the Mountain

Storm King Mountain looks peaceful and quiet. But in 1994, a fire on Storm King Mountain killed 14 firefighters.

The fire was burning on a canyon slope. Fifty-two firefighters were called to fight it. They attacked the fire from below and above the slope. Then, disaster struck.

The wind changed. Flames jumped from one side of the canyon to the other. The flames set fire to heavy brush on the bottom of the opposite slope. The firefighters were trapped between two walls of fire!

Some firefighters used fire shelters to hide. Others took cover on patches of burned-out ground. The rest tried to race the fire up a steep slope to safety. Fourteen firefighters didn't make it. One of them was smokejumper Don Mackey. He had gone back to lead others to safety. He died trying.

---

fire shelter: fire-resistant material that firefighters wrap around themselves when they have no other way to escape a fire
patch: a small area

Mann Gulch—a Death Trap

On August 5, 1949, a fire started in Helena National Forest, Montana. The fire was burning along a ridge. The area was hard to reach. An 18-person smokejumping crew flew in.

Once on the ground, the crew headed down into Mann Gulch. The wind was at their backs. The fire was burning along a ridge on the other side of the gulch.

As the crew got close to the bottom of the gulch, the wind changed direction. Now it was blowing toward them. It blew embers over the gulch. The embers started a fire just beneath the crew. The fire was now racing up toward them!

When the group saw the fire coming, they turned around and started back up the hill. But the area was mostly grass and scrub. The fire moved fast.

---

gulch: a deep valley that fills with water when it rains
embers: the hot, glowing remains of a fire
scrub: low bushes or short trees

William Dodge, the crew leader, saw the fire might catch them. He lit an escape fire to burn a patch for shelter. He laid down in the hot patch. When the main fire reached the burned patch, there was no fuel for the fire to burn. Dodge suffered burns, but he lived.

The rest of the crew did not understand what Dodge was doing. Two firefighters went straight up the steepest hill and over the ridge. They lived. The others ran up the hill as well. But the fire caught them. All 15 died.

But lessons were learned. On August 29, 1985, 75 firefighters were trapped in a similar firestorm. This was at Butte, Idaho, in the Salmon National Forest. Most of the crew reached safety through planned escape routes. But some crew members did not plan well and made mistakes. They still had to use fire shelters.

---

firestorm: a fire over a large area with high winds

Trapped on Higgins Ridge

On August 4, 1961, 12 smokejumpers parachuted to a fire in Montana's Nez Percé Forest. Eight other jumpers also had dropped in earlier.

Strong winds were blowing. The fire raged out of control. Then the wind changed. The fire began to spread in the opposite direction. The smokejumpers became trapped. "The fire exploded like a blowtorch," one jumper said later.

The two crews looked for safety on a burned-out section. Some took their shirts and soaked them in water. They wrapped the wet shirts around their heads for protection.

Soon flames surrounded them. The winds blew at 50 miles (80 kilometers) per hour. The firefighters were in deadly danger.

rage: to burn violently
blowtorch: a tool that blows a very hot flame
protection: something that keeps you from harm

Helicopter Hero

A helicopter appeared from the smoke clouds above. The pilot, Rod Snider, had spotted the jumpers' orange shirts. He had come to rescue them. Snider carried the jumpers to safety.

For the last three trips, two jumpers rode in the cabin. Two others rode outside, holding on to the skids.

For his bravery, Snider was awarded the North American Forest Service medal. He also received the Stanley Hiller Jr. Pilot of the Year Award.

---

skids: two bars on which the helicopter sits on the ground

Too Good a Job?

Smokejumpers successfully put out many fires. But some people think this can make other fires worse.

Every area of forest burns once every 50 to 100 years. Left alone, a fire will burn itself out. But what if there are homes or offices nearby? A fire cannot be left to destroy them.

Wildfires also destroy animal habitats. They burn timber and brush. Loss of plant life causes erosion. Wildfires also create smoke, which can hurt people's health. So smokejumpers fight to control wildfires.

But stopping fires creates another danger. An unburned forest now can grow older. Trees will get taller. Plants will get thicker. Next time a fire starts, there will be more to burn.

Fires can even have positive effects. For example, soil from burned forest areas is rich in nutrients. Might this be another reason to let some fires burn?

---

erosion: the slow wearing away of land by wind or water
habitat: the area where a plant or animal grows or lives
nutrient: something that plants need to stay healthy

Trying to Help

People need more facts about forests and wildfires. Meanwhile, smokejumpers will continue to do their jobs. They will continue to risk their safety to protect our homes. They will continue to leap from planes to save nature's beauty from deadly forest flames.

Firefighters battle a blaze.

Epilogue

Scientists want to learn more about how fires behave. Some scientists use computers to model weather patterns that cause wildfires. Other scientists use special maps that tell what kinds of trees grow in an area. Some trees burn more quickly or easily than others. So these maps can help people guess how fast a fire may spread.

This sort of data can be very helpful in fighting wildfires. Smokejumpers can use science as another tool to battle the forest flames.

model: to act like
data: information; facts

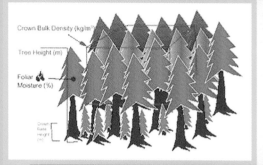

Software helps scientists to predict how certain trees might burn in a forest fire.

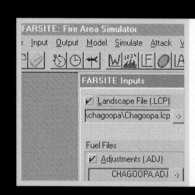

Scientists can also use computers to do "pretend burns." This allows them to test their ideas about how certain trees burn.

The computer can even create special maps to help scientists "see into" places they cannot visit.

43

Glossary

aerial: from the air
agriculture: farming of all types
apprehensive: highly aware
blowtorch: a tool that blows a very hot flame
calisthenics: a type of exercise to make certain parts of the body stronger
candidate: someone who wants to join a group
cargo: things carried by a truck, plane, train, or ship
chemical: a substance used in chemistry
citizen: a person who belongs to a named country
confidence: belief in your abilities
conscientious objector: a person who refuses to do something because his or her beliefs forbid it
data: information; facts
drought: a severe lack of rain
embers: the hot, glowing remains of a fire
erosion: the slow wearing away of land by wind or water
experimental: something that has not yet been fully tested
fireline: land specially prepared to stop a fire from spreading
fire retardant: a chemical that slows the advance of a fire
fire shelter: a fire resistant material that firefighters wrap around themselves when they have no other way to escape a fire
firestorm: a fire over a large area with high winds
focus: to aim rays of light through a lens
focused: thinking only about one thing
forestry: working with trees, woodlands, and forests
fuel: something that gives heat or power by burning
gulch: a deep valley that fills with water when it rains
habitat: the area where a plant or animal grows or lives
historic: a past event that is seen as important
hot spots: areas where roots under the soil are burning
humidity: the amount of water vapor in the air
jumpsuit: a suit that parachute jumpers wear
kevlar: a special fireproof material
malice: a desire to hurt someone or something
medical: anything to do with health and medicine
mission: a special job or task
model: to act like

Nomex: a material that can stand heat

nutrient: something that plants need to stay healthy

obstacle: something that gets in your way or prevents you from doing something

pack-out test: a test to carry a heavy load over a distance

parachute: a long piece of fabric attached to thin ropes

pass: the act of going, by, beyond, over, or through

patch: a small area

physical: anything to do with the body

portable: able to be carried or moved easily

professional: someone who is paid to do a job that requires special training

protection: something that keeps you from harm

qualify: to reach a level that allows you to do something

rage: to burn violently

rappel: to use ropes to let yourself down from a high place

reserve: spare; backup

rookie: a person who is new to a job

scrub: low bushes or short trees

simulator: a machine that gives you an experience that is like the real thing

skids: two bars on which the helicopter sits on the ground

snag: to catch or grab

spotter: the person in command of a smokejumper team

spur: a spike on the heel or bottom of a boot

static line: a rope that opens the parachute as a jumper leaps from a plane

streamer: a long piece of narrow paper that is rolled up

tactic: a means to reach a goal

target: a mark to aim at

temporary: not lasting; having an end

trek: to walk across difficult ground

trip line: a rope or cord used to open a latch on a door

veteran: a person who served in the military

Bibliography

Beil, Karen Magnuson. *Fire in Their Eyes: Wildfires and the People Who Fight Them.* San Diego: Harcourt Brace, 1999.

Greenberg, Keith Elliot. *Smokejumper: Firefighter from the Sky.* Risky Business. Woodbridge, Conn.: Blackbirch Press, 1995.

Salas, Laura Purdie. *Forest Fires.* Natural Disasters. Mankato, Minn.: Capstone Press, 2002.

The Smokejumper. The National Smokejumper Association's magazine (formerly called *The Static Line).* Published four times a year.

Useful Addresses

National Interagency Fire Center
3833 S. Development Avenue
Boise, ID 83705–5354

National Smokejumper Association
NSA Membership
10 Judy Lane
Chico, CA 95926–1714

USDA Forest Service
P.O. Box 96090
Washington, DC 20090–6090

Internet Sites

National Smokejumper Association
http://www.smokejumpers.com/

The National Wildland/Urban Interface Fire Program
http://www.firewise.org/

Spotfireimages.com
http://www.spotfireimages.com/

USDA Forest Service
http://www.fs.fed.us/

Index